250

The Stuff Dreams Are Made Of.

Proudly supplying the equipment that helps the
dreams of future champions come true. Since 1884.

Louisville Slugger®

Louisville Slugger®

BOSTON
RED SOX

DICK LALLY

BONANZA BOOKS

New York

First published in 1991 by Bonanza Books, distributed by Outlet Book
Company, Inc., a Random House Company, 225 Park Avenue South,
New York, New York 10003, by arrangement with MBKA.

Louisville Slugger is a registered trademark
of Hillerich & Bradsby Company, Louisville, Kentucky

This book has not been authorized by, and is not an official publication
of, the Boston Red Sox. The views represented are those of the author.

ACKNOWLEDGMENTS

Majority of Player Photographs by Tom Dipace
Additional thanks to:
John Broggi—JKJ Sports Collectibles, Inc.
National Baseball Hall of Fame & Museum, Inc.

Printed and bound in the United States of America

Library of Congress Cataloging-in-Publication Data

Lally, Dick.
    The Boston Red Sox / by Dick Lally.
        p.   cm. — (Louisville Slugger)
    Summary: An overview of the Boston Red Sox baseball team,
discussing its history, last season, great moments, records, and
prospects.
    ISBN 0-517-05790-5
    1. Boston Red Sox (Baseball team)—Juvenile literature.
[1. Boston Red Sox (Baseball team)] I. Title. II. Series.
GV875.B62L33 1991
796.357′64′0974461—dc20   90-28329
                                      CIP
                                       AC

ISBN 0-517-05790-5

8 7 6 5 4 3 2 1

CONTENTS

JOE MORGAN
MANAGER

Prior to 1988 Morgan was a career minor league manager. He worked in the Pirate system from 1966 to 1973 and joined the Boston organization in 1974. He took over the helm of the Red Sox on July 14, 1988, and immediately revived a club that had stagnated under John McNamara. He enjoyed the best managerial start in baseball history, as his team won its initial 12 games and 19 of its first 20. Prior to that streak the Red Sox had looked like a second-division club, but they overtook the front-running Detroit Tigers and won the AL East. Morgan was the Man of the Year in Boston despite a playoff loss to Oakland. The following year he began to hear the boos, as the club struggled through a mediocre season. Morgan's moves — strategies that are often based on nothing more than gut feeling — were criticized by fans, media, and some players. He survived the sniping in 1990 to lead Boston to another AL East title. This one was even more impressive than the first. His team's offense was crippled by injuries and the free-agent defection of Nick Esasky. Its pitching staff came out of spring training looking like Clemens, Boddicker, and pray for rain and a hurricane. Club speed was nonexistent. Yet Morgan somehow held it all together, and the Red Sox won. He used three unknown quantities (Harris, Bolton, and Kiecker) to complete his starting rotation, and he nursed his way through the season's most crucial part with virtually no bullpen.

DANNY DARWIN

PITCHER

One of the most sought after players in the 1990 free agent sweepstakes, Darwin signed with the Red Sox on December 19. He first came to the major leagues as a Texas Ranger in 1978. For his first two full years with Texas, Darwin was used chiefly as a long reliever. He won 12 games in that role while notching an additional victory as a starter in 1980. It was thought that his overpowering fastball would make him an ideal closer. However, over the next five and a half seasons, Darwin spent most of his time in the starting rotations of the Rangers and the Milwaukee Brewers. He was traded to the Astros in the middle of the 1986 season. A 5-2 record with that club contributed to Houston's division title. Darwin has pitched consistently well throughout his career but he has been victimized by poor run support. He notched only one winning season (1986) from 1983 to 1988, but his luck began to change in 1989 when he was primarily used in long relief again. His 11-4 record that season gave him the best winning percentage on the Astros. Darwin began 1990 as a reliever, but Houston eventually found a spot for him in the starting rotation as the right-hander enjoyed his finest season. He repeated his 11-4 mark for a club that finished below .500. His 2.21 ERA led the National League and was a career best. In 1991 Darwin is expected to step into the Red Sox rotation, though he is also fine insurance if Jeff Reardon's back troubles him again.

Age: 35		Bats: Right							Throws: Right	
	W	L	SV	G	CG	IP	HA	BB	SO	ERA
1990	11	4	2	48	3	162.2	136	31	109	2.21
Career	111	109	29	488	47	1913	1777	580	1265	3.40

MATT YOUNG

PITCHER

The signing of Matt Young was one of several that raised the bile of many major league owners. It is easy to understand why. The Red Sox rewarded Young with a three-year $6.35 million contract despite his underwhelming statistics. Young enters the 1991 campaign with a career record that is 27 games below .500. He has won only nine games in the last three seasons. His 12 wins in 1985 are a single-season high. However, there was some justification for the signing. The Red Sox were desperate for starting pitching. Young's 8-18 record last season was largely the result of poor run support. His other numbers were quite impressive. Despite pitching in a notorious hitters' park, the left-hander's 3.51 ERA placed him in the American League's top 15. His 176 strikeouts were good for eighth place. The Sox were especially desirous of acquiring an "inning-eater," a workhorse who could save wear and tear on the bullpen. Young's 225⅓ innings pitched in 1990 qualifies him for the role. It was the eighth best total in the circuit. But the Red Sox should have some concern about his health. Injuries drastically curtailed his playing time in 1988 and 1989. They also should wonder whether he will be effective in Fenway Park. Young is a hard-throwing lefty. Southpaws who changed speeds and kept the ball down (e.g., Bill Lee and Mel Parnell) have had the greatest success on Boston's home turf.

Age: 32				Bats: Left					Throws: Left	
	W	L	SV	G	CG	IP	HA	BB	SO	ERA
1990	8	18	0	34	7	225.1	198	107	176	3.51
Career	51	78	25	264	19	956.0	971	413	666	4.26

TOM BOLTON
PITCHER

The Red Sox waited 10 years for this left-hander to fulfill the expectations they had when they signed him out of high school in the 1980 June draft. Bolton showed flashes of brilliance in his minor league career, but he was unable to translate that into big league success. For instance, he was an impressive 12-5 with a 2.89 ERA with Pawtucket in 1989. Those numbers won him a promotion to the Red Sox on August 2. But the minor league magic apparently left his arm, and he lost all four of his starts and posted an 8.31 ERA. It marked the third consecutive year Bolton had disappointed the Red Sox after a call-up. He wasn't even expected to make the club's starting rotation in 1990. At best, he was viewed as a left-handed mop-up man or a backup to Rob Murphy. But injuries and Boston's lack of left-handed starters gave his career a positive spin. With a third of the season over, the Red Sox pressed him into a starting role almost out of desperation—and he responded with the best season of his career. His 3.38 ERA was a major league career best, and his 10-5 record gave him one of the best winning percentages in the league. The 10 wins were also tenth among American League left-handers. He pitched excellent relief in a losing cause after replacing Roger Clemens in the second inning of the final game of the AL playoffs.

Age: 28			Bats: Left						Throws: Left	
	W	L	SV	G	CG	IP	HA	BB	SO	ERA
1990	10	5	0	21	3	119.2	111	47	65	3.38
Career	12	12	1	82	3	229	250	98	144	4.21

ROGER CLEMENS
PITCHER

Has the Rocket had too many launchings too early in his career? For the past five seasons, Clemens has been arguably the best pitcher in baseball. Unlike his closest competitors for that title—Dwight Gooden and Dave Stewart—Clemens pitches in a park that is unkind to pitchers. Until shoulder stiffness shelved him for part of last season, he was posting his best numbers since 1986, the summer he won the first of two consecutive Cy Young Awards. Clemens was dominating in 1990. He led the AL in ERA (1.93, the first sub-2.00 ERA by a Red Sox pitcher since 1972) and tied for the league lead in shutouts (4, with Stewart). The injury probably kept him from wrestling away Nolan Ryan's strikeout title. It also underlines a disturbing pattern. Despite his overwhelming success, Clemens has broken down in each of the last three seasons. He has thrown a large number of pitches in a relatively brief time. Such abuse has been known to dim even the brightest of flamethrowers by the time they were 30. There is also some concern that he may be too high-strung. Clemens punched a door with his right (pitching) hand when he discovered the division-clinching party would not be held without the media present. Whether or not he should have been ejected from the final game of the AL playoffs is moot. No ace should ever put himself in a position where he can be run from such a crucial contest. The Red Sox have to be concerned.

Age: 28			Bats: Right					Throws: Right		
	W	L	SV	G	CG	IP	HA	BB	SO	ERA
1990	21	6	0	31	7	228.1	193	54	209	1.93
Career	116	51	0	206	65	1513	1281	425	1424	2.89

RANDY KUTCHER

OUTFIELD

Kutcher epitomizes perseverance. He was originally signed by the San Francisco Giants in the 1979 June draft. He spent seven years (1979–85) in the Giants' farm system without enjoying a major league at-bat. The reason? Kutcher was a singles hitter with excellent speed but little power. His minor league batting averages were underwhelming, and he rarely walked. His means of survival was his versatility. He was an excellent outfielder, and he could competently play all four infield positions. As a seven-year minor leaguer, he was granted free agency in October 1985, but he re-signed with San Francisco on February 3, 1986. The club took him to spring training that year. He failed to make the major league roster, but a .346 start coupled with a surprising 11 home runs at triple-A Phoenix won him a June 18 promotion to San Francisco. He batted just .237 with the Giants but managed to hit 7 home runs in only 186 at-bats. Despite the aberrant power outburst, Kutcher failed to win a regular spot with the Giants. On December 9, 1987, he was sent to Boston as the player-to-be-named later in the Dave Henderson trade. After playing most of 1988 with triple-A Pawtucket, Kutcher spent the 1989 season with Boston as a valuable utility man. He played five different positions, including one game as a catcher, and made only three errors. He batted .299 with men in scoring position. Kutcher continued to provide Boston with bench strength in 1990.

Age: 30		Bats: Right						Throws: Right		
	G	AB	H	2B	3B	HR	R	RBI	SB	AVG.
1990	63	74	17	4	1	1	18	5	3	.230
Career	244	448	102	25	6	10	83	40	13	.228

WES GARDNER
PITCHER

Wes Gardner came to Boston along with Calvin Schiraldi as part of the deal that put Bobby Ojeda on the Mets. It was a good deal for both clubs. Bobby O has helped pitch the Mets to a world championship and a division title. The Red Sox wouldn't have reached the 1986 World Series without Calvin Schiraldi, and Wes Gardner contributed to their 1988 AL East title. Gardner went 8-6 with a 3.50 ERA that summer and was hailed as a young pitcher with a bright future. However, the last two years have been unkind. A sore right elbow put him on the 21-day disabled list from May 21 to June 21, 1989. He returned to the club but never regained his form. On August 27 a ball hit by Tiger infielder Mike Brumley struck Gardner below the right eye. Surgery was performed to repair several broken bones, and Gardner was sidelined for the remainder of the year. In 1990 the club mistakenly placed his name instead of Jeff Reardon's on the 15-day disabled list. When he did appear on the mound, it was obvious that he was still struggling to find himself. He was briefly used in the bullpen, but that experiment was abandoned with the arrival of Larry Andersen. Gardner's 1990 record was unimposing, but it also held some reasons for optimism. His 58 strikeouts in only 77⅓ innings are evidence that his arm is once again sound. Steady work may be all he needs to turn his career around.

Age: 29			Bats: Right					Throws: Right		
	W	L	SV	G	CG	IP	HA	BB	SO	ERA
1990	3	7	0	34	0	77.1	77	35	58	4.89
Career	18	29	13	172	1	440.1	444	204	346	4.84

GREG HARRIS

PITCHER

Boston's Cinderella Man in 1990. Prior to last season, Harris had started only one game in the previous two years. The bullpen had been the scene of his greatest triumphs. In 1986 he was one of the best relievers in baseball, as he posted 20 saves and a 2.83 ERA for the Texas Rangers. In 111⅓ innings pitched he struck out 95 batters. For some baffling reason, the Rangers used him as a starter the following season, and he lost twice as many games as he won. In 1988, as a Philadelphia Phillie, he was one of the best long relievers in baseball. He continued that success after coming over to Boston as a free agent on August 7, 1989. So it was something of a surprise when he was pressed into the starting rotation in 1990. Injuries to John Dopson and Wes Gardner necessitated the move. Harris responded with a career-high 13 wins. His 117 strikeouts in 184⅓ innings were third on the club behind Clemens and Boddicker. On August 26 he and Jeff Gray combined to give Boston its third consecutive shutout of the Toronto Blue Jays. It was the first time since 1962 that a Red Sox pitching staff had engineered three straight whitewashings. Harris did appear to tire toward the end of the season. Depending on the shape of the starting rotation in 1991, he could be back in the bullpen as set-up man to Jeff Reardon. His final role will largely depend on the health of Jeff Reardon and John Dopson and the status of Larry Andersen.

Age: 35			Bats: Right					Throws: Right		
	W	L	SV	G	CG	IP	HA	BB	SO	ERA
1990	13	9	0	34	1	184.1	186	77	117	4.00
Career	48	54	38	417	2	975.1	886	421	743	3.61

DANA KIECKER
PITCHER

The way Tom Bolton and Dana Kiecker pitched for Boston last season was reminiscent of the way Lynn McGlothen and John Curtis pitched for the Red Sox in the 1972 pennant race. Kiecker played a vital role in the Red Sox flag drive despite his losing record. He literally came from out of nowhere to make his contribution. He had been in the Boston organization for six years and had posted a winning record in only two seasons. He spent all of 1989 in Pawtucket, and his 8-9 record with 163 hits allowed in 147 innings pitched would not have ordinarily merited much attention. However, Kiecker was a six-year renewal free agent at the end of that season. After the Red Sox signed him in December, they had to carry him on the team's 40-man roster. It was Kiecker's first time on the major league roster, and he made the most of the opportunity. He pitched his way onto the club during spring training. By mid-season he was part of the regular rotation. Kiecker won only eight games, but he pitched well enough to win several more. Though he lost three consecutive starts in September, he did some of his best pitching in Boston's biggest games. He first beat the Blue Jays on June 19. Then on August 24 he combined with Jeff Gray to shut out Toronto and up the Boston lead to two games. In the AL playoffs against Oakland, he pitched 5⅔ innings and surrendered only one earned run. He left the contest with a no-decision.

Age: 30			Bats: Right					Throws: Right		
	W	L	SV	G	CG	IP	HA	BB	SO	ERA
1990	8	9	0	32	0	152	145	54	93	3.97
Career	Rookie year—career statistics same as above.									

DENNIS LAMP
PITCHER

During his 14-year major league career, Dennis Lamp has performed a variety of roles. You can sum up his job description with the simple word "pitcher." As a starter with the Chicago Cubs, he won in double figures twice and pitched a one-hitter against San Diego in that pitcher's nightmare called Wrigley Field. During the strike-shortened 1981 season he became a swingman for the Chicago White Sox. Alternating between the bullpen and the starting rotation, Lamp pitched well enough to place third in the AL ERA standings. On August 25 of that year he pitched his second career one-hitter. In 1983 the White Sox made him their primary stopper. He responded with a career-high 15 saves, as Chicago won the AL West. On January 10, 1984, he was signed as a free agent by the Toronto Blue Jays. They used him almost exclusively in long relief. He went 11-0 in his first season with the club. His pitching suffered in 1986 and 1987. He was released by both the Blue Jays and the Oakland A's. He was signed to a triple-A contract by Boston on Janury 5, 1988. It was a worthwhile gamble for the Sox. Lamp was a valuable long reliever on the division-winning team of 1988 and pitched even better in 1989. In both years he acted as the right-handed set-up man for Lee Smith. He was not as good last season, partially because injuries in the pen left him with a less defined role. He pitched long relief, acted as a closer, and even started a game.

Age: 38			Bats: Right					Throws: Right		
	W	L	SV	G	CG	IP	HA	BB	SO	ERA
1990	3	5	0	47	0	105.2	114	30	49	4.68
Career	89	92	35	567	21	1711	1842	509	785	3.87

ROB MURPHY

PITCHER

Prior to 1990 Murphy had put together a solid major league career. The Cincinnati Reds made him a first-round pick in the secondary phase of the 1981 January draft. After five years in the minors, he made the big leagues for good in 1986. Working as the primary left-handed set-up man for Reds' bullpen ace John Franco, Murphy had a 6-0 record with an eye-popping 0.72 ERA. In 50⅓ innings pitched he surrendered a paltry 26 hits. Left-handers found Murphy particularly baffling. They hit only .133 against him. He continued to excel in the set-up role in 1987 and 1988. During trade talks at the winter meetings, clubs made an annual attempt to pry him loose from the Reds. Boston finally succeeded by trading Todd Benzinger, Jeff Sellers, and Luis Vasquez to Cincinnati for Murphy and Nick Esasky. The trade was a boon for Boston. Esasky was the club's top slugger in his only year with the team, and Murphy had a sterling year in the bullpen. Setting the table for Lee Smith, he saved nine games of his own and became the first Red Sox reliever to strike out 100 or more batters since Mark Clear in 1982. 1990 was his first off-season. Murphy got off to a dismal start and never seemed able to work his way out of it. He was prone to surrendering the long ball at inopportune moments. Murphy's arm is apparently sound, and that bodes well for a comeback. He is a fine fielder. He has yet to make an error in the major leagues.

Age: 30			Bats: Left						Throws: Left	
	W	L	SV	G	CG	IP	HA	BB	SO	ERA
1990	0	6	7	68	0	57.0	85	32	54	6.32
Career	19	24	23	391	0	400.2	370	166	371	3.17

JEFF REARDON

PITCHER

Jeff Reardon signed with Boston as a free agent on December 6, 1989. The Red Sox gave him a three-year, $6.8 million contract despite an off-year with the Minnesota Twins in 1989. Reardon did save 31 games that season, but he also had 11 blown saves, and his ERA was a less than stellar 4.07. A chronic sore back contributed to his sub-par performance. It also kept him on the disabled list for a good part of 1990. As a result, Reardon went nearly two months between saves (July 20 to September 27). The drought-ending save came against Detroit and put Boston in first place on the eve of their final series with Toronto. The next evening he shut down the Jays and got credit for the win. He also saved both the tie-clinching and division-clinching victories against the Chicago White Sox. Despite the time missed, he led the team with 21 saves. This made him the only active pitcher with nine consecutive seasons of 20 or more saves. His 287 career saves places him fourth behind Rollie Fingers (341), Rich Gossage (307), and Bruce Sutter (300) on the all-time list. He is the only pitcher in major league history to record 30 or more saves in five straight seasons (1985-89). He is also the only pitcher to record 40 or more saves in each league. In 1989 he was named the Rolaids Relief Man of the Decade. His 31 saves for the Twins in 1987 helped make them World Series winners.

Age: 35			Bats: Right					Throws: Right		
	W	L	SV	G	CG	IP	HA	BB	SO	ERA
1990	5	3	21	47	0	51.1	39	19	33	3.16
Career	62	65	287	694	0	943.1	796	320	755	3.03

JOHN MARZANO
CATCHER

Marzano has been in the Boston organization since signing as a first-round draft pick in the 1984 June draft. That summer he hit .333 as a member of the U.S. Olympic baseball team. When that squad went on its pre-Olympic tour, Marzano led all hitters with a .407 batting average, which included 11 extra-base hits. Those stats combined with his exceptional record at Temple University (.409, 22 home runs, 141 RBIs in 115 games played over three years) made Marzano the most highly touted young catcher in the country. He hit only .246 in his first year of pro ball (New Britain, 1985). That average was deceptive, since he batted .275 over the final three months of the season. He batted .283 for that same club in 1986 and seemed on his way to stardom, as he led the team in doubles and RBIs. In 1987 he looked ready for the major leagues. He had 10 home runs in only 255 at-bats with Pawtucket when his contract was purchased by the Red Sox on July 30. Boston's starting catcher, Rich Gedman, had been placed on the DL, and the team needed a replacement. Marzano filled in capably, and he showed excellent power (11 doubles and 5 home runs in only 168 at-bats). He started the 1988 season with Boston, hit badly, and was sent back to the minors. In 1989 he played only seven games with the Red Sox. The remainder of his season was spent in Pawtucket. Last season he got into 32 games as Tony Pena's backup. He may need a change of scenery in order to live up to the earlier expectations.

Age: 28		Bats: Right							Throws: Right			
	G	AB	H	2b	3B	HR	R	RBI	BB	SO	SB	BA
1990	32	83	20	4	0	0	8	6	5	10	0	.241
Career	101	298	73	19	0	6	36	34	13	56	0	.245

TONY PENA
CATCHER

Pena represented one of the more astute free-agent signings of last season. He signed a Red Sox contract on November 27, 1989. With the mysterious decline of former All-Star Rich Gedman, Boston's catching had been a weakness for three years. Pena turned it into a strength. He brought a reliable bat to what had been an out spot in the lineup. His hitting, however, was a bonus. Pena's greatest contributions to Boston were defensive. He was the anchor of the league's most surprising pitching staff. Displaying an almost uncanny ability to call a game, Pena guided Tom Bolton, Greg Harris, and Dana Kiecker to the best seasons of their careers. Even veterans Clemens and Boddicker benefited from his counsel. As a hitter, Pena continued to belt the line drives that have become his trademark. His walk total (43) was the second highest of his major league career. Equipped with a powerful arm, Pena kept opposing base runners honest throughout the season. He is the master of the snap throw to first base. Pena also brought an intangible value to the clubhouse. He has long been one of baseball's most enthusiastic competitors. His presence infused the Red Sox with a camaraderie that previous clubs had been missing. During a late-season losing streak, with the division slipping away, Pena launched into a tirade, blasting his teammates' lackadaisical effort. Feelings were bruised—but the team got the message.

Age: 33			Bats: Right						Throws: Right		
	G	AB	H	2b	3B	HR	R	RBI	BB	SO	SB	BA
1990	143	491	129	19	1	7	62	56	43	71	8	.263
Career	1350	4676	1275	212	23	89	500	528	321	590	67	.273

JACK CLARK
FIRST BASE/DESIGNATED HITTER

On December 15 American League pitchers discovered that Jack the Ripper would spend 1991 in Fenway Park. In choosing the Red Sox as a new look free agent, Clark was giving himself an opportunity to play in a hitters' park for the first time in his career. The slugger first entered the major leagues as a San Francisco Giant in 1975. Since then his home addresses have included Candlestick Park, Busch Memorial Stadium, Yankee Stadium, and Jack Murphy Stadium. None of these parks were conducive to Clark's style of hitting. Despite this, he has managed to gather 307 home runs and a 1,060 RBI in an injury-plagued career. Clark is one of baseball's most powerful hitters. Playing in Fenway, with its cozy dimensions and inviting left field wall, the slugger could have a career year similar to Andre Dawson's MVP 1987 season with the Chicago Cubs. Besides being a dangerous hitter, Clark is an intense competitor and one of the most bruising base-runners in the game. His final numbers will be affected by two variables: his ability to readjust to American League pitching and his health. Clark has missed at least 30 games in five of the last seven seasons. With this in mind, it would probably be best if the Red Sox utilized him as a designated-hitter. He performed in that role for the Yankees in 1988 and appeared in 150 games for only the third time in his career.

Age: 34			Bats: Right					Throws: Right		
	G	AB	H	2B	3B	HR	R	RBI	SB	AVG.
1990	115	334	89	12	1	25	59	62	4	.266
Career	1773	6109	1652	303	38	307	1011	1060	76	.270

WADE BOGGS
THIRD BASE

The hitting machine showed some wear and tear in 1990. For the first time since joining the Red Sox in 1982, Boggs went into the final week of the season in jeopardy of not hitting .300. His .302 was the lowest mark of his big league career, and his lowest professional average since he hit .263 in his initial minor league season with Elmira. His 87 walks were also a career-low for a full major league season. In 1989 Boggs became the first major leaguer to achieve four consecutive seasons with 200 hits and 100 walks. He was also the first modern-era major leaguer to post seven straight 200-hit seasons. For five consecutive seasons he led the AL in on-base percentage, and for seven straight years he scored 100 or more runs. All four streaks came to an end in 1990. Yet it was still a performance most nonslugging types would gladly accept. Boggs's 187 hits were second highest in the league. His 44 doubles placed him one behind the two league leaders, teammate Jody Reed and batting champion George Brett. Boggs still lacks home-run power. His 24 homers in 1987 must now be viewed as an abberation. However, when healthy—and he wasn't for most of last season—he is among the very best at setting the table for his team's RBI men. When he first came to the league, he was a man without a position, seemingly lost at first, at third, and in the outfield. But he has turned himself into one of the best third basemen in the majors.

Age: 32			Bats: Left						Throws: Right			
	G	AB	H	2B	3B	HR	R	RBI	BB	SO	SB	BA
1990	155	619	187	44	5	6	89	63	87	68	0	.302
Career	1338	5153	1784	358	41	70	912	586	841	407	14	.346

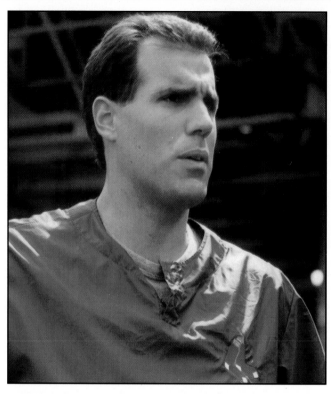

MIKE MARSHALL
OUTFIELD/FIRST BASE

Marshall would probably like to forget the last two seasons. In 1988 he had one of his most productive seasons. His 20 home runs and 82 RBIs helped bring a world championship to the Los Angeles Dodgers. But in 1989 a chronic back problem, which had limited his playing time in 1986 and 1987, plagued him once again. He appeared in only 105 games, and old whispers of malingering were revived. After the season he was traded with pitcher Alejandro Pena to the New York Mets for Juan Samuel. Marshall's short tour with the Mets was no smoother than his final season with L.A. He was handed the first baseman's job in spring training, a move that ruffled the feathers of Dave Magadan. Though he won some early games with his bat, Marshall failed to hit with consistency, and his defense was sub-par. Then he went on the disabled list. With the Red Sox desperate for offense in a tightening pennant race, they made a deal for Marshall late in the season. He did not join the club immediately. He was on the DL from July 16 to July 28 with a gastrointestinal inflammation. He then did a rehab stint with Pawtucket and joined the Red Sox in late August. His biggest hit of the season came on August 24. His ninth-inning RBI single was the game-winning blow in a Dana Kiecker–Jeff Gray shutout of Toronto. On September 8 he had three hits, as he helped lead Boston to a 10-2 route of Seattle. At his best, he drove in 95 runs for the 1985 Dodgers.

Age: 31		Bats: Right					Throws: Right					
*	G	AB	H	2B	3B	HR	R	RBI	BB	SO	SB	BA
1990	83	275	71	14	2	10	34	39	11	66	0	.258
Career	1011	3524	953	169	8	147	429	523	247	790	26	.270

*Includes NL statistics with the Mets.

TIM NAEHRING

SHORTSTOP

This rookie made a powerful impression in a short time. Had it not been for injuries, he might even have won the full-time shortstop job. Naehring has been in the Red Sox organization since 1988. His climb through the system has been rapid. In his first year in the minors, he was a co-winner of Boston's Tony Latham Memorial Award, an honor given each fall to the Red Sox minor leaguer who displays the most enthusiasm during the Florida Instructional League season. In 1989 a .301 start at Lynchburg (209 at-bats) won Naehring a promotion to triple-A Pawtucket, where he hit .275 and drove in 31 runs in only 273 at-bats. In his first triple-A at-bat, he doubled off Ron Guidry, who was on a rehabilitation assignment with Columbus. Naehring's numbers caught the attention of the Red Sox brass. Boston writers voted him the Red Sox Minor League Player of the Year, and he was invited to spring training in 1990. He was restricted to only 85 at-bats with the big league club, but he showed a good batting eye and excellent power for a middle infielder. Naehring possesses good range at short, but he has to cut down on his errors. In 1989 he made 33 in 135 games. That was actually an improvement over his 26 errors in 61 games in 1988. His fielding continued to improve in 1990. The Red Sox had an erratic offense last season. If Naehring displays competence in the field, he could be the starting shortstop in 1991.

Age: 24				Bats: Right					Throws: Right		
	G	AB	H	2B	3B	HR	R	RBI	BB	SO	SB	BA
1990	24	85	23	6	0	2	10	12	8	15	0	.271
Career	Rookie year—career statistics same as above.										

CARLOS QUINTANA
FIRST BASE

Quintana's 0-for-13 against the Oakland A's in the AL playoffs dampened what had been a solid season. Despite the large collar, the first baseman did manage to drive in Boston's only run in a 4-1 second-game loss. Signing Quintana was something of a gamble for Boston. A .208 hitter in 1989, he was given the first-base job virtually by default after the free-agent defection of slugger Nick Esasky. Quintana responded with a season that was similar to the productive summers he had spent in the minor leagues. Though he couldn't duplicate Esasky's power, he was a dependable gap hitter who brought line-drive doubles to the Boston offense. Manager Joe Morgan used Quintana in the number two spot for most of the season. The Red Sox would like to see more home runs from him, but his minor league record makes no promise of power. Fenway Park is a home-run haven, yet Quintana did not hit his first Fenway homer until June 26. He did help the club with a number of clutch hits. On September 7 he drove in the tying run in the ninth inning and the winning run in the eleventh of a game against Seattle. The Sox were coming off three consecutive losses and couldn't have afforded a fourth. Though he wouldn't make any excuses for his poor playoff performance, Quintana did play throughout September with a sore right shoulder, which hampered his swing. With Phil Pantier and Mo Vaughan emerging, Quintana may have to beef up his RBI totals to stay in the lineup.

Age: 26			Bats: Left						Throws: Right		
	G	AB	H	2B	3B	HR	R	RBI	BB	SO	SB	BA
1990	149	512	147	28	0	7	56	67	52	74	1	.287
Career	188	595	165	33	0	7	63	75	61	89	1	.277

JODY REED
SECOND BASE/SHORTSTOP

Syd Thrift thought Reed was Boston's MVP in 1990. The second baseman was his team's most reliable hitter throughout a season in which most of his mates endured lengthy slumps. Reed's five home runs, a career high, did not place him among the league's elite sluggers, but his 45 doubles tied him with Kansas City's George Brett for the AL lead. At least one of Reed's home runs was memorable. On June 25 he homered in the sixth inning against the Toronto Blue Jays, who had won fifteen consecutive games at Fenway. The blast severed a 7-7 tie and enabled Boston to end that embarrassing streak. It also set the tone for the remaining contest between the two clubs. When he is not clouting the rare home run, Reed is the best bunter on the team and an adept hit-and-run man. His 51 RBIs were a career high. Detroit's Lou Whitaker was the only AL second baseman to drive in more. With his 75 walks, Reed was often used by Joe Morgan as a leadoff hitter. He does not steal bases, but he is a superb base runner. Reed has been a model of consistency throughout his major league career. In three full seasons with Boston, Reed has never hit lower than .288 or higher than .293 (he hit .300 in 30 at-bats in 1987). He seems to have found a comfortable niche. In the final game of the 1990 AL playoffs, Reed drove in his team's only run against Dave Stewart. The status of Luis Rivera, Tim Naehring, and Marty Barrett will determine if Reed will be Boston's shortstop or second baseman in 1991.

Age: 28		Bats: Right							Throws: Right			
	G	AB	H	2B	3B	HR	R	RBI	BB	SO	SB	BA
1990	155	598	173	45	0	5	70	51	75	65	4	.289
Career	419	1490	432	111	4	9	210	127	197	130	10	.290

LUIS RIVERA
SHORTSTOP

Rivera joined Boston in July 1989, when incumbent second baseman Marty Barrett was forced on the disabled list with a right knee injury. Shortstop Jody Reed moved to second and Rivera assumed the duties at short. He and Reed have been Boston's main double-play partners ever since. Rivera's strength is his glove. He is occasionally error-prone, but he compensates for it with excellent range. His defense was shaky during the 1990 season's final month. His sixth-inning error in the third game of the AL playoffs opened the door for an Oakland rally. As a hitter, he hasn't progressed much since his minor league days, when he struggled to reach .250. However, he has shown some surprising flashes of power. For example, in 1985 he hit 16 home runs while playing for Jacksonville. Last season he hit 7 home runs in 346 at-bats. His 45 RBIs were a most respectable figure, considering his playing time and position. Rivera has been especially productive against Boston's arch-rivals, the New York Yankees. In his first Red Sox start (June 10, 1989), he hit a home run in Yankee Stadium. One month later he faced the Yankees again—and hit a home run and two doubles, for a career-high eight total bases. In 1990 Rivera continued to pick on the Bronx Bombers. On August 31 he hit the first grand slam of his career, off Yankee reliever Jeff Robinson. The four runs provided the margin of victory in a 7-3 win. He may have to hit more to remain a regular.

Age: 27		Bats: Right							Throws: Right			
	G	AB	H	2B	3B	HR	R	RBI	BB	SO	SB	BA
1990	118	346	78	20	0	7	38	45	25	58	4	.225
Career	407	1238	283	67	5	16	128	118	87	228	10	.229

ELLIS BURKS
CENTER FIELD

Does anyone remember that at the start of spring training, 1990, there were rumors that Burks would be shipped to the New York Mets for Ron Darling and Juan Samuel? Can anyone imagine that Boston might have been crazy enough to pull the trigger on that deal? Burks has been the franchise's best talent since joining the club on April 29, 1987, and last year he was its best player. Playing for a club whose offense has been in decline for the last three years, Burks hit .296 while leading the team in home runs (21), triples (8), and RBIs (89) and tying for the team high in runs (89). He hit two home runs in one inning on August 27. In the field, he continued to show the grace that has invited comparisons to perennial Gold Glover Paul Blair. The only part of Burks's game that was off was stolen bases. In 1987 he was the first Red Sox rookie to hit 20 home runs and steal over 20 bases. His 27 steals that year were the second highest by a rookie in Red Sox history (Tris Speaker stole 34 in 1909). In 1989 he became the first Red Sox player since Tommy Harper (1972-74) to record three consecutive seasons of 20 or more stolen bases. Last year, however, he pilfered only nine bags while getting caught 11 times. Apparently, getting caught stealing early in the season made him run-shy for the rest of the summer. Boston needs someone to jump-start their offense, so Burks will probably return to running form in 1991.

Age: 26			Bats: Right						Throws: Right		
	G	AB	H	2B	3B	HR	R	RBI	BB	SO	SB	BA
1990	152	588	174	33	8	21	89	89	48	82	9	.296
Career	526	2085	606	119	21	71	349	301	187	321	82	.291

TOM BRUNANSKY
OUTFIELD

When Bruno joined Boston as part of the early-season trade that sent Lee Smith to the St. Louis Cardinals, it was thought that the cozy dimensions of Fenway Park would revive his power stroke. Brunansky was one of four active players with 20 or more home runs in each of the previous eight seasons. After all, he had hit 20 for St. Louis in 1989 while playing in a ballpark that is inhospitable to the long ball. A regular dose of Fenway was expected to return him to the 30-plus level he had twice achieved with the Minnesota Twins. This was not the case. Brunansky had spent two years away from the American League, and it took him some time to reacclimate himself to AL pitching. By August 11 he had gathered only eight home runs in a Boston uniform (he had hit one with the Cardinals). But he made up for the early lack of power in a big way. On September 29, after having driven in only 11 runs in his previous 38 games, Bruno hit three home runs in a game against the Toronto Blue Jays. He was red-hot that weekend, as Boston took two out of three from its closest pursuers. During that crucial series, Brunansky hit five home runs. Teammate Dwight Evans later said, "Bruno made it look as if he were playing slo-pitch softball this weekend." Brunansky provided further heroics in the field. His game-saving catch for the last out against the White Sox on the last day of the season helped clinch the division title.

Age: 30		Bats: Right							Throws: Right			
	G	AB	H	2B	3B	HR	R	RBI	BB	SO	SB	BA
1990	148	518	132	27	5	16	66	73	66	115	5	.255
Career	1376	4943	1227	232	25	224	659	712	606	903	63	.248

MIKE GREENWELL

LEFT FIELD

By the end of the 1989 season, the Red Sox were comparing Greenwell to the great hitters of the game. By the middle of the 1990 season, they were talking about trading him. Ankle injuries had seemingly retarded his growth as a hitter. Greenwell got off to a horrific start, joining his teammates in an offensive malaise. To help ward off the "evil spirits" that had obviously possessed the Boston bats, Greenwell held a mystic ritual in the Red Sox clubhouse. It must have worked. His bat heated up in August and was scorching in September. Greenwell hit .370 that month, as the Red Sox held off the Blue Jays. Unlike Jose Canseco, Cecil Fielder, and Mark McGwire, Greenwell is a contact hitter with extra-base power. Like teammate Wade Boggs, he is hard to strike out and becomes a more dangerous hitter as the pitcher goes deeper into the count. Green-well's weakness is his defense. He has limited range and is prone to misplay. However, he does have a strong, accurate arm. His lack of speed often results in double plays, yet he is a heady base runner who can steal a base in crucial situations. He finished second to Jose Canseco in the 1988 MVP voting. That was his best season, as he was named to the UPI, *Sporting News, Baseball America,* AP Major League, and American League All-Star teams and won a *Sporting News* Silver Bat. Despite his slow start last year, he finished fourth in the league in hits. When healthy, he can contend for a batting title.

Age: 27		Bats: Left									Throws: Right	
	G	AB	H	2B	3B	HR	R	RBI	BB	SO	SB	BA
1990	159	610	181	30	6	14	71	73	65	43	8	.297
Career	635	2256	707	139	20	73	326	388	251	176	43	.313

KEVIN ROMINE
OUTFIELD

Romine is one of those players you don't readily notice, but he has immense value to the Red Sox. He joined the Boston organization as a second-round pick in the 1982 June draft. His rise up the minor league ladder was slow. After reaching triple-A in his third professional season, Romine was stuck at Pawtucket for the better part of four years. He did see some time in Boston during that period, but he failed to get 100 big league at-bats in any single season until 1989. He was hitting .300 when his contract was purchased on June 8. Serving as a backup at all three outfield positions, Romine hit .274 while making only three errors. He was batting .311 as late as August 2, but a hand injury put him in an average-deflating 6-for-72 slump. He finished strong and batted .338 in his final 21 games. Romine proved that 1989 was no fluke by providing a steady offensive contribution off the Boston bench in 1990. He has been especially effective against left-handed pitching and is one of the club's better hitters with a runner in scoring position. In addition, he is one of the few Red Sox blessed with speed. Because of this, Romine is especially treasured by the Red Sox. He can be used as a pinch runner and defensive replacement, and he is the only player on Boston's current major league roster who can adequately spell Ellis Burks in center field.

Age: 29		Bats: Right								Throws: Right	
	G	AB	H	2B	3B	HR	R	RBI	BB	SO	SB	BA
1990	70	136	37	7	0	2	21	14	12	27	4	.272
Career	287	575	149	28	1	4	82	48	46	114	10	.259

1990 SEASON

Baseball prognosticators have learned to shatter their crystal balls when it comes time to peek into the future of the Boston Red Sox. Prior to the 1986 season, for example, the Red Sox were universally picked to finish as also-rans. They came within an out of winning the World Series. Then, the 1987 club was expected to contend, if not repeat as league champions. It finished below .500. The Red Sox were largely overlooked in 1988's pre-season polls, and their performance before the All-Star break seemed to justify this. However, a torrid final three months of the season carried them to a division title. They contended in 1989, but that was due more to the inadequacy of their division rivals than to Boston's strength. That club struggled most of the summer and barely finished above .500.

Only the most rabid Red Sox devotee believed the team would contend in 1990. Its ace, Roger Clemens, had seemed painfully mortal during stretches of the 1989 season. It was whispered that the more than 1,000 innings the Rocket had pitched in four years had exacted a heavy toll and that his magic arm would never again be the fearsome piece of artillery it had been in the past. A sub-par Clemens would all but eliminate the pitching-bereft Red Sox from contention.

Clemens's possible physical limitations weren't the only clouds in the Boston pennant picture. The Red Sox were a relatively old club as the 1990 campaign began. Only three of the regulars—short-stop Jody Reed, left fielder Mike Greenwell, and center fielder Ellis Burks—were less than 30 years

old. Boston's most potent run producer, right fielder Dwight Evans, would be 39 before 1990 ended.

The aging offense was also hampered by the free-agent defection of first baseman Nick Esasky. Esasky had led the 1989 Red Sox in home runs (30) and RBIs (108). He had finished fourth in the AL with a .500 slugging percentage. The Red Sox wanted to re-sign him, but they were outbid by the Atlanta Braves. Boston responded with two free-agent signings of its own. It picked up reliever Jeff Reardon from the Minnesota Twins and catcher Tony Pena from the St. Louis Cardinals. Boston's catching had been woeful since the unexpected decline of Rich Gedman in 1987. Pena was expected to shore up the club's defense and guide the shaky pitching staff. Though not a power hitter, he would bring a reliable bat to the lineup.

The signing of Reardon gave Boston a wealth of stoppers in the bullpen. Reardon had saved at least 20 games in each of the previous eight seasons. No other pitcher could make that claim. He had been a primary force behind Minnesota's world championship in 1987. Though he had been off his usual form in 1989, he had still managed to save 31 games.

The Red Sox already had a super closer in big Lee Smith. The powerful right-hander had racked up 25 saves of his own in 1989 and had struck out 96 batters in only 70 $\frac{2}{3}$ innings. No one believed that Reardon and Smith would last the season together. It was obvious that Smith would be shopped. He was in the final year of his contract, and despite his effectiveness, his aching knees would limit his playing time. The smart money wagered that he would be dealt for the starting pitcher Boston desperately needed.

The smart money was wrong. Smith and Reardon started the season as teammates. In fact, Smith assumed the lion's share of the early work, as a bad back curtailed Reardon's efforts. By the time Reardon was ready to assume more of the burden, Boston was no longer interested in trading Smith for a starter. Its rotation was still woefully thin, but another, more crying, need had developed. The Red Sox offense was near collapse.

Hitting machine Wade Boggs got off to the worst start of his career. Mike Greenwell seemingly forgot how to hit. Dwight Evans, the rock of the Red Sox offense for a decade, was disabled by a sore back. Second baseman Marty Barrett continued a three-year offensive slide that was aggravated by a 1989 knee injury. Pena and first baseman Carlos Quintana hit and shortstop Jody Reed usually found a way to get on base, but they didn't have the power to jump-start an offense. Only center fielder Ellis Burks remained a consistent offensive force.

Faced with this dilemma, Boston traded Lee Smith to the St. Louis Cardinals for outfielder Tom Brunansky. Bruno was coming off eight consecutive seasons of 20 or more homers, and he had always played well in Fenway Park when he was with the Minnesota Twins.

At first, the acquisition seemed to have little impact. The Boston situation worsened when Reardon's back ailments returned and intensified, putting him on the disabled list. The Red Sox were now forced to do battle with a pitching staff consisting of only two reliable hurlers (Roger Clemens and Mike Boddicker) and an offense bereft of power and speed. Had they been in any other division, they could have packed up and gone home for the summer.

Fortunately, they were in the AL East, the least powerful circuit in baseball. Though their record remained less than overwhelming, the Red Sox never strayed far from contention. They stayed in or near the division's top spot until just before the All-Star break, and then they became the hottest team in baseball.

Surprisingly, starting pitching and defense were the keys to their revival. Boston clubs are usually renowned for their heavy-hitting squads, but this club suffered a power shortage throughout the summer. It did, however, get hits when it counted most, and an unexpectedly fine performance by its starters made the most of whatever runs the team scored. Roger Clemens pitched like the Rocket of old until an inflamed shoulder sidetracked him in early September. Mike Boddicker was an excellent number two. However, the rotation got its biggest boost from three unexpected starters: 34-year-old career reliever Greg Harris, the previously unheralded Tom Bolton, and 29-year-old rookie Dana Kiecker. In Reardon's absence, various pitchers filled in as the closer. Boston had trouble spelling relief, but the late August acquisition of right-hander Larry Andersen from the Houston Astros did give the Sox at least one reliable arm in the bullpen.

The pitchers were aided by a defense that tightened as the season matured. A six-game winning streak at the start of August pushed them into first place. A ten-game winning streak had Boston 6 ½ games ahead of second-place Toronto on September 3. That streak included three consecutive shutouts of the Blue Jays (August 24–26) by Kiecker, Clemens, and Harris. But then the season began to unravel. Roger Clemens aggravated his right shoulder while losing to Dave Stewart and the Oakland A's on September 4. The Red Sox would lose 10 of their next 15 games, while the Blue Jays surged. By the end of the day on September 19, Toronto led Boston by a full game.

On September 28, the two teams were tied as the Blue Jays came to Fenway for a three-game series. Boston took the first contest, a Friday night affair won by Jeff Stone's first hit of the season. The next day, the Rocket made a dramatic return, starting his first game in more than three weeks. Firing on all cylinders, the Boston ace shut Toronto out for six innings, as the Red Sox won again. A Sunday victory for the Blue Jays kept matters close. The division would not be settled until the final day, when a Tom Brunansky circus catch sealed Mike Boddicker's victory over the Chicago White Sox. The Red Sox were champions of the AL East!

But then they met the Oakland A's.

Tony Pena

HISTORY

Competing in a sporting climate in which "nice guys finish last" and "winning isn't everything—it's the only thing," the Boston Red Sox have often found that their many notable achievements have been ignored. That's unfortunate, because this is one of baseball's most celebrated and successful franchises.

They were not always known as the Red Sox. When Boston came into the American League as a charter member in 1901, the team was simultaneously referred to as the Americans, the Pilgrims, the Puritans, the Plymouth Rocks, and the Somersets. Fans finally settled on the Pilgrims.

The team was an immediate success. Jimmy Collins, the best third baseman in the game at the time, was brought in as player manager. Also lured to the team were some of the rival National League's top stars, including future Hall of Famer Cy Young and slugger Buck Freeman. The powerful assemblage was a contender in its first two seasons and then ran away with the pennant in 1903. It finished with a 14½-game margin over second-place Philadelphia. More importantly, it defeated Pittsburgh in the first modern World Series. That victory legitimized the AL as a truly major league.

The club repeated in 1904 when New York Highlander ace Jack Chesbro's wild pitch gave Boston the pennant on the next to last day of the season. There was no Series that year; the National League's New York Giants refused to play.

The next few years marked a transition period for the club. The old stars were gradually discarded and fresh talents, such as future Hall of Famer Tris Speaker and fireballing right-hander Joe Wood ("There's no man alive can throw the ball harder than Smokey Joe Wood."—Walter Johnson) were added to the roster. Now known as the Red Sox, the team played respectable ball from 1909 to 1911. It was during this time that Duffy Lewis and Harry Hooper joined Speaker to form baseball's greatest defensive outfield. The infield was shored up when Steve Yerkes was installed at second, allowing second baseman Larry Gardner to switch to third base. Gardner excelled at his new position.

Fenway Park opened in 1912. The timing was excellent. Led by the miraculous arm of Smokey Joe Wood (34-5) and the hitting of Speaker (.383) and Gardner (.315), the Red Sox took the pennant by 14 games. This time the New York Giants did not ignore their Series invitation. With Joe Wood winning three games and striking out 21 batters in 22 innings, the Red Sox won their second world title.

Joe Wood's broken thumb relegated the club to fourth place in 1913, but they were an American League power for the remainder of the decade. The Red Sox finished second in 1914 and 1917—and took the top spot in 1915, 1916, and 1918, winning the World Series in each of those years. By the end of the 1918 season, they were considered a juggernaut. The club's regular nine contained a healthy blend of veterans and young talent. The pitching staff was not only the best in the major leagues, it was also the youngest. A further period of domination seemed to be Boston's future.

But then the dark days set in.

Boston owner Harry Frazee was a Broadway producer who had suffered a run of bad luck. Desperate for money to prop up his shows, he dismantled his great club, selling his top stars after a disappointing sixth-place finish in 1919. The most infamous of these deals was the sale of Babe Ruth to the New York Yankees on January 3, 1920.

Ruth, who joined Boston as a 19-year-old rookie in 1914, had become the team's biggest attraction. For a time he was the league's best left-handed pitcher. However, his slugging talents were so prodigious that he gradually insinuated himself into the regular lineup as an outfielder. Even hitting only part-time, Ruth won a home-run title in 1918. With increased use in 1919, he set a major league home-run record (29). Ruth's bat kept fans flocking to Fenway despite his team's mediocre season. His sale to the Yankees underscored Boston's complete collapse. The Red Sox would spend the next 15 seasons in the second division.

Millionaire Tom Yawkey, a Red Sox fan to his marrow, bought the club in 1933 and tried to immediately resuscitate it. He opened his wallet wide and bought such stars as Joe Cronin, Jimmie Foxx, Lefty Grove, Max Bishop, Rube Walberg, and Wes Ferrell. They lifted the club back into the first division, but they failed to win a pennant. However, the veteran acquisitions did allow the Red Sox to field a respectable team while rebuilding with youth. Starting in the late 1930s, a battalion of talent led by Hall of Famers Ted Williams and Bobby Doerr swelled the Boston roster. The Red Sox became a contender and finally won the pennant in 1946, though they lost the World Series to the Cardinals and Enos Slaughter's mad dash to home plate.

A distant third-place finish in 1947 failed to discourage the team. From 1948 to 1950 the Sox were engaged in three of the hottest pennant races in American League history. Boston nearly took the 1948 flag. Tied on the season's final day, they lost a single-game playoff to Lou Boudreau and the Cleveland Indians. The following year they were 12 games behind the Yankees on July 4. Winning at a torrid pace from that point on, they took a one-game lead into the final two-game series against hated New York. The Joe DiMaggio–led Bronx Bombers won both contests and the pennant. In 1950 a late season slump left them four games behind New York.

It was the team's last attack of pennant fever until

Carl Yastrzemski

1967. That season, led by young manager Dick Williams, Triple Crown MVP Carl Yastrzemski, and Cy Young Award winner Jim Lonborg, the Red Sox shocked all of baseball. A ninth-place club in 1966, they took first place after the most spirited pennant race in league history. They then lost a hard-fought World Series to the St. Louis Cardinals in seven games.

Since that "Impossible Dream" pennant of 1967, the Red Sox have been one of the league's most powerful clubs. Unlike the woeful times following the sale of Ruth, Boston has been below .500 only three times in the last 24 seasons. It won the pennant in 1975 and 1986. On both occasions the Red Sox took their Series opponents to seven thrilling games before succumbing. Because of a fluke caused by a strike-shortened schedule, the club finished only half a game behind the division-winning Tigers in 1972. Two and a half games separated it from the top in 1977. In 1978 Boston narrowly missed another title when it lost a single-game playoff to the New York Yankees. Though picked by some experts to finish in the second division, the Sox did win a division title in 1988, though they lost the playoffs to the Oakland A's. This club may have suffered some heart-breaking losses in its time, but no one could ever call it a loser. As the 1990s opened up, Boston continued to be a force in the American League.

The Rocket Soars: Roger Clemens strikes out a major league record 20 Seattle Mariners (April 29, 1986)

BATTING

Ellis Burks

Games .... Mike Greenwell   159

At-bats .... Wade Boggs   619

Batting average .... Wade Boggs   .302

Runs .... Wade Boggs, Ellis Burks   89

Hits .... Wade Boggs   187

Doubles .... Jody Reed   45

Triples .... Ellis Burks   8

Home runs .... Ellis Burks   21

On-base percentage .... Wade Boggs   .386

Slugging percentage .... Ellis Burks   .486

RBIs .... Ellis Burks   89

Total bases .... Ellis Burks   286

Walks .... Wade Boggs   87

Most strikeouts .... Tom Brunansky   105

Stolen bases .... Ellis Burks   9

Caught stealing .... Ellis Burks   11

1990 TEAM LEADERS

PITCHING

Roger Clemens

Games .... Rob Murphy   68
Wins .... Roger Clemens   21
Losses .... Greg Harris, Dana Kiecker   9
Starts .... Mike Boddicker   34
Complete games .... Roger Clemens   7
Shutouts .... Roger Clemens   4
Innings .... Roger Clemens   228
ERA .... Roger Clemens   1.93
Strikeouts .... Roger Clemens   209
Walks .... Greg Harris   77
Saves .... Jeff Reardon   21
Relief appearances .... Rob Murphy   68
Winning percentage ..... Roger Clemens   .778
Hits allowed .... Mike Boddicker   225

1990 TRANSACTIONS

DATE	PLAYER	TRANSACTION
January 9	Dana Kiecker	Purchased from Pawtucket
January 10	Shane Rawley	Signed as free agent
March 28	Josias Manzanillo	Reassigned to minor league camp
	Pedro Matilla	Reassigned to minor league camp
	Phil Plantier	Reassigned to minor league camp
April 2	Steve Ellsworth	Placed on waivers for unconditional release
	Shane Rawley	Placed on waivers for unconditional release
	Rob Woodward	Placed on waivers for unconditional release
April 3	Scott Cooper	Optioned to Pawtucket
	Steve Curry	Returned to Pawtucket
	Angel Gonzalez	Returned to Pawtucket
	Joe Johnson	Returned to Pawtucket
	Tim Naehring	Returned to Pawtucket
April 6	Bill Buckner	Purchased from Pawtucket
	Billy Jo Robidoux	Purchased from Pawtucket
	Tom Bolton	Optioned to Pawtucket
	Eric Hetzel	Optioned to Pawtucket
April 13	John Leister	Purchased from Pawtucket
	Wes Gardner	Placed on 15-day disabled list (elbow)
April 19	Eric Hetzel	Recalled from Pawtucket
	John Leister	Optioned to Pawtucket
April 20	Daryl Irvine	Recalled from Pawtucket
	Mike Rochford	Outrighted to Pawtucket
April 28	Wes Gardner	Reinstated from the disabled list
	John Trautwein	Purchased from Pawtucket
	John Dopson	Placed on 15-day disabled list (elbow)
	Billy Jo Robidoux	Placed on 15-day disabled list (shoulder)
April 29	John Marzano	Optioned to Pawtucket
April 30	Daryl Irvine	Optioned to Pawtucket
May 3	Jerry Reed	Signed as free agent from Seattle
	John Trautwein	Optioned to Pawtucket
May 4	Tom Brunansky	Obtained from St. Louis in exchange for Lee Smith
May 14	John Dopson	Assigned to Pawtucket on injury rehabilitation
June 4	John Dopson	Reinstated from the disabled list
	Eric Hetzel	Optioned to Pawtucket
June 5	Jeff Gray	Purchased from Pawtucket
	Bill Buckner	Placed on waivers for unconditional release
June 7	John Marzano	Recalled from Pawtucket
	Rich Gedman	Traded to Houston for a player to be named later
June 13	Tom Bolton	Recalled from Pawtucket
	John Dopson	Placed on 15-day disabled list
June 28	Billy Jo Robidoux	Reinstated from the disabled list
	Danny Heep	Placed on 15-day disabled list (slipped disc)
	John Dopson	Transferred to 21-day disabled list
July 15	Tim Naehring	Purchased from Pawtucket
	Dwight Evans	Placed on 15-day disabled list (back/hamstring)
July 28	Mike Marshall	Acquired from Mets for minor leaguers Greg Hansell, Ender Perozo and player to be named later
	Billy Jo Robidoux	Outrighted to Pawtucket
July 30	Dwight Evans	Reinstated from the disabled list
	Randy Kutcher	Optioned to Pawtucket

DATE	PLAYER	TRANSACTION
July 31	Joe Hesketh	Signed as free agent
	Wes Gardner	Placed on 15-day disabled list (sore elbow)
August 3	Daryl Irvine	Recalled from Pawtucket
	Jeff Reardon	Placed on 21-day disabled list (disc surgery)
August 10	Rick Lancellotti	Purchased from Pawtucket
	Mike Marshall	Optioned to Pawtucket
	John Dopson	Assigned to Pawtucket on injury rehabilitation
August 12	Wes Gardner	Reinstated from the disabled list
	Jerry Reed	Placed on waivers for unconditional release
August 20	Mike Marshall	Recalled from Pawtucket
	Rick Lancellotti	Optioned to Pawtucket
	Phil Plantier	Recalled from Pawtucket
	Tim Naehring	Placed on 15-day disabled list
August 21	John Leister	Outrighted to Pawtucket
	John Trautwein	Outrighted to Pawtucket
August 24	Rick Lancellotti	Outrighted to Pawtucket
August 31	Randy Kutcher	Recalled from Pawtucket
	Phil Plantier	Optioned to Pawtucket
	Larry Andersen	Acquired from Houston for Jeff Bagwell
	Daryl Irvine	Optioned to Pawtucket
September 2	Danny Heep	Reinstated from the disabled list
September 4	Scott Cooper	Recalled from Pawtucket
	Daryl Irvine	Recalled from Pawtucket
	Phil Plantier	Recalled from Pawtucket
	Billy Jo Robidoux	Purchased from Pawtucket
	Jeff Stone	Purchased from Pawtucket
September 8	Eric Hetzel	Recalled from Pawtucket
September 12	Jeff Reardon	Reinstated from the disabled list
September 15	Jim Pankovits	Purchased from Pawtucket
October 23	Tom Brunansky	Filed for free agency
October 24	Mike Boddicker	Filed for free agency
October 28	Danny Heep	Filed for free agency
October 29	Dwight Evans	Placed on waivers for unconditional release
	Jim Pankovits	Placed on waivers for unconditional release
October 31	Tom Fischer	Promoted to 40 man roster
	Derek Livernois	Promoted to 40 man roster
	Dan O'Neill	Promoted to 40 man roster
	Dave Owen	Promoted to 40 man roster
	Jeff Plympton	Promoted to 40 man roster
	Scott Taylor	Promoted to 40 man roster

Tom Brunansky

1991 ASSESSMENT

Dewey is gone. It is difficult to imagine the Red Sox without Dwight Evans effortlessly tossing out errant base runners from right field or driving in yet another Boston run. His October 25 release severed his team's, and the public's, last visible link to the 1975 World Series. It was sad. It was also necessary. In 1990 Evans hit 10 of his 13 home runs in Fenway Park, a sure sign that his power was waning. With the Red Sox hoping to re-sign Tom Brunansky, and with Mo Vaughn and Phil Plantier waiting in the wings, Evans's playing time was already in jeopardy. It has also been written (by Mike Geffner in his Rundown column in *The Village Voice*) that Dewey and manager Joe Morgan were not on the best of terms.

How will the Red Sox be without Evans? It is hard to predict. Boston has confounded the experts for the last 20 years. It wins when it shouldn't and loses when everyone thinks it should win. That said, this club will probably have a hard time repeating, even in a weak division.

They have too many question marks, far more than a division-winning club ought to have. With the free-agent defection of Mike Boddicker, the pitching staff is unsettled after Roger Clemens. Will Matt Young survive in Fenway—a ballpark most lefthanders view as a locale for *Nightmare on Elm Street*? Can Kiecker, Bolton, and Harris repeat their performances of 1990? Until they do there will be ample cause for skepticism. And if they do, it might not be enough unless Clemens repeats his stellar campaign and Young replaces Boddicker's 17 wins. That is asking a lot. Clemens, in particular, must be viewed warily, as he continues to be plagued by late-season arm woes. If that shoulder ever breaks down, the next sound you'll hear will be Fenway Park sliding into the Charles River. Boston simply can't contend without him.

It has been a long time since Boston has had to shore up its offense, but the truth of the matter is the offense isn't nearly as potent now as it has been in the past. The Red Sox don't run, they don't move runners over, and for a team that plays half of its games in Fenway Park, they don't hit with nearly enough power. That is a problem that can be corrected internally. A healthy Greenwell can add about 10 home runs to his total, and both Mo Vaughn and Phil Plantier hit their share of long balls in the minors. With Evans gone, the re-signing of Brunansky, who could hit 30 home runs, is crucial.

It is also crucial that the Red Sox bullpen be realigned. If Jeff Reardon can stay pain-free for most of the season, the pieces should easily fall into place. There is enough proven talent in the pen to make this a team strength. However, if Reardon goes down again or somehow falters, this club doesn't have anyone capable of replacing him.

The infield poses another sizable question for Boston. If Naehring wins the starting shortstop's job, it should give Boston an additional serviceable bat. The infield is bereft of power, and this could put Quintana's first-base slot in jeopardy.

The Red Sox are a team with a plethora of questions—about as many questions as they faced at the start of the 1988 and 1990 seasons. They won division titles in both those years, so they cannot be discounted. Boston often finds a way to surprise everyone.

PROSPECTS

PHIL PLANTIER
Outfield

This muscular 22-year-old outfielder started his career in the Red Sox chain as a singles-hitting third baseman. His glove was a liability, so he was moved to the outfield in the middle of the 1988 season. He also added 25 pounds of muscle to his frame and began to hit the ball for distance. In 1989, while playing for Lynchburg of the Carolina League (A), Plantier led the league in home runs (27), slugging percentage (.546), total bases (242), and RBIs (105) while batting .300. He also finished second in hits (133) and third in runs scored (73). *Baseball America* was impressed enough to name him the Class A Player of the Year, and he was named the Carolina League's MVP.

That performance persuaded Boston to invite Plantier to its major league spring training camp in 1990. He batted .500 (6 for 12) with five RBIs and won advancement to Boston's triple-A club, the Pawtucket Red Sox of the International League. Plantier hit only .253 and led the league with 148 strikeouts. However, he also hit 33 home runs and collected 79 RBIs. These numbers are deceptive. Plantier was overmatched at first, but he made great strides in the second half of the season. In his last twelve minor league games, the left-handed batter hit 10 home runs. That hot streak won him an August 20 call to Boston. Red Sox general manager Lou Gorman expects Plantier to compete for a full-time job with the big club in 1991.

MAURICE VAUGHN
First Base

At 6'1″ and 225 pounds, he is known as Big Mo. Vaughn, a left-handed hitter, graduated from Trinity Pawling Prep in Pawling, New York, and attended Seton Hall University. His record at Seton Hall was impressive. His three-year varsity average was .417, and he drove in 218 runs. Vaughn's 57 career home runs are a Seton Hall record. His 28 home runs as a freshman first baseman are also a school record. At the end of his college career, he was named Big East Player of the Decade. He was chosen by the Red Sox as their second pick in the first round of the 1989 June draft (24th pick overall).

The Red Sox were so excited by Mo's potential they had him bypass A ball and assigned him to New Britain of the double-A Eastern League. Mo rewarded their confidence by hitting .278 with 8 home runs and 38 RBIs in only 245 at-bats (73 games). In 1990 he continued his progress with Pawtucket. He was his team's best all-around hitter. He batted .295 with 22 home runs and 72 RBIs. He's an odds-on favorite to crack Boston's regular lineup (probably as a DH) in 1991.

SCOTT COOPER
Third Base

The Red Sox have a wealth of third base prospects. Not bad for a team that already has a hitting machine and Gold Glove candidate at the position. Cooper has been the Boston minor league player most coveted by other teams when it comes time to talk trade. The 23-year-old left-handed hitter graduated from Pattonville High School (St. Louis) in 1986 and was picked by the Red Sox in the third round of that year's June draft. He was signed by scout Don Lenhardt. Cooper immediately reported to Elmira of the Class A New York–Penn League. He drove in 43 runs in only 51 games while batting .288 and leading the team in home runs (nine). In 1987 he played 119 games for Greensboro (.251, 15 home runs, 63 RBIs in 119 games).

Despite his low batting average, his progress as a power hitter marked him as a player to watch. He was assigned to Lynchburg in the highly competitive Carolina League (A) in 1988. In what was considered a pitcher's league, Cooper became an all-star third baseman by leading the league in doubles (45) and total bases (324) while tying for the league lead in hits (148). His .298 batting average was the eighth highest in the circuit.

Those statistics won him a 1989 promotion to New Britain in the Eastern League (double-A). He got off to a horrendous start. By the end of June he was batting only .217 and had shown little of the power he had exhibited in other minor league stops. His bat started to come around in mid-August, and he raised his average to a final .247 while leading the club in hits (104), doubles (24), runs (50), and RBIs (39). That finish pushed Cooper to Pawtucket (triple-A) in 1990, and he put together a solid season (.266, 12 home runs). His stroke is tailor-made for Fenway Park, but there are still some holes in his game. He needs to be more selective at the plate. Cooper doesn't walk enough and his fielding needs polish. Cooper has good range, but he has also been error-prone throughout his minor league career.

The August trade of the highly touted Jeff Bagwell, also a third baseman, to the Houston Astros for reliever Larry Andersen, makes Cooper's path to a major league job that much clearer.

OTHER RED SOX PROSPECTS TO WATCH

The Red Sox are desperate for pitching help. Despite the presence of Roger Clemens, they have one of the older pitching staffs in the major leagues. Even rookie Dana Kieker will be 30 before the start of the 1991 season. There is some help available in the minor leagues. Mike Dalton (7-4, 2.55 at Pawtucket) is a left-handed reliever whose strength lies in his uncanny control. He lacks that one nasty strikeout pitch that all closers need, but he could make the big club as a left-handed long reliever in 1991.

Tom Fischer, Derek Livernois, and Dan O'Neill (New Britain) probably won't see Fenway until 1992, though a hot spring and the shaky status of the Red Sox pitching staff could prompt an earlier call-up. Fischer (13-10, 4.19) is a left-handed starter with excellent control and a good breaking pitch. The Red Sox are short on left-handed starters, and this is to Fischer's advantage. The right-handed Livernois (9-2, 1.98) is a power pitcher who gets the ball over the plate. O'Neill (7-0, 0.72) is a left-handed reliever who has even better control than his two teammates. Unlike the aforementioned Mike Dalton, O'Neill can strike batters out. He probably needs a summer at Pawtucket, but he is clearly Boston's best pitching prospect. Should Dalton falter, O'Neill could make the Red Sox in 1991.

Maurice Vaughn

Phil Plantier

KEY TRANSACTIONS

For years Red Sox owner Tom Yawkey tried to "buy" a pennant for Boston. He often found the financially strapped Philadelphia A's to be willing accomplices. On December 12, 1933, Boston acquired Lefty Grove, Rube Walberg, and Max Bishop from the A's for Bob Kline, Rabbit Warstler, and $125,000. The trade did not bring Yawkey the pennant he had hoped for, but it did put some color back in the cheeks of an ailing franchise. Bishop and Walberg had little impact on the club; both were past their prime. Grove nursed a sore arm through his first Boston season and was lucky to eke out a .500 record (8-8). His next five seasons, however, were sensational. He won four ERA titles (an unheard-of feat for a left-hander in Fenway Park) and led the AL in winning percentage in 1939 (.789). During this five-year stretch, Grove won 83 games while losing only 41.

The A's and Red Sox continued their chummy relationship on December 10, 1935, when Boston obtained Jimmie Foxx and John Marcum from Philadelphia for Gordon Rhodes, George Savino, and $150,000. This trade did not produce a pennant winner or even a contender. But it did provide the Red Sox with a super slugger worthy of showcasing while the team was being rebuilt. It also signaled that the front office would go to any expense to reverse the team's fortunes. In six full years with Boston, Foxx won one home-run title, an RBI championship, and a batting title. He led the league in slugging twice. The first baseman also protected the young Ted Williams in the Red Sox lineup.

Ironically, it was a relatively minor deal that helped bring Yawkey his much desired pennant. On January 3, 1946, the Red Sox traded Eddie Lake to Detroit for Rudy York. It was not the sort of deal that captures major headlines. Eddie Lake was a 30-year-old journeyman shortstop with decent speed and an excellent batting eye. York was a 33-year-old slugger in decline. All the trade did was clinch the 1946 AL flag for the Red Sox. York played the best first base of his career that summer and was the slugger the lineup needed to protect Ted Williams. York drove in 119 runs and combined with Williams and Doerr to form the most productive trio in the majors.

Their old friends the A's were bereft of talent throughout most of the 1930s and '40s, so Boston turned to another cash-short franchise for pennant help. On November 17, 1947, it received Junior Stephens and Jack Kramer from the St. Louis Browns for Roy Partee, Jim Wilson, Al Widmar, Ed Pellagrini, Pete Layden, Joe Ostrowski, and $310,000. Vern (Junior) Stephens wasn't a great shortstop (though he wasn't nearly so bad a fielder as some would suggest), but he sure could crack that apple. The AL RBI leader during the Browns' pennant-winning season of 1944, Stephens made an already strong Boston lineup terrifying. He drove in 440 runs in his first three seasons with the Sox, and Boston was a contender in each of those years. Almost as a bonus, Kramer led the league in winning percentage (.783) his first year in Boston. This was a large trade for the time, and it got larger the next day, when Boston got Ellis Kinder and Billy Hitchcock from the Browns for Sam Dente, Clem Dreisewerd, Bill Sommers, and $65,000. This may have been the best transaction of the two-day tradefest. Kinder was 34 years old, and few believed there was much life left in his arm. But that arm was good enough to win 47 games during his first three years with the Sox, most of which were spent as a starter. In 1951 Kinder went to the bullpen and became the best reliever in the American League. He led the league in saves that year (14) and again in 1953 (27).

The perennially contending Red Sox went into a decline from the mid-1950s to late 1960s. One of their few bright spots during this period was provided in another trade with a weak franchise. On December 9, 1953, Boston received Jackie Jensen from the Washington Senators for Mickey McDermott and Tom Umphlett. Jensen, a golden-haired, 27-year-old outfielder, seemed to be cursed with unlimited promise that hadn't quite found its expression during his first four major league seasons with the Yankees and Senators. That changed as soon as he donned a Red Sox uniform. In his first year with the team, he drove in 117 runs and led the league with 22 stolen bases. He drove in 550 runs in

the next five years, leading the league three times. He was the AL MVP in 1958 and a Gold Glove winner in 1959.

Pitching was usually a weakness for the Red Sox. Two deals that centered around pitching helped boost Boston to its 1975 pennant. The first was the signing of Luis Tiant. There was no fanfare when this former 20-game winner signed with the Red Sox in 1971. A sore arm had plagued him for three years, and most observers thought he was finished. His first season with the Sox (1-7, 4.88) seemed to confirm this view. But Tiant would win the ERA title in 1972 and become the ace of the Red Sox pitching staff. In seven full seasons with the club (1972–78), El Tiante won 121 games while losing only 74. Not bad for someone who hadn't even cost a player in return. He was the ace of the pennant-winning 1975 club.

Another key pitcher on that squad, Rick Wise, came to the Red Sox from the St. Louis Cardinals with outfielder Bernie Carbo on October 26, 1973. The price was Reggie Smith and Ken Tatum. This was a good deal for both clubs. Smith would provide the Cardinals with much-needed power for the next two years. Injuries held back the right-

Luis Tiant

handed Wise in his first year with Boston, but he was a 19-game winner for the 1975 AL champs. Carbo was a valuable left-handed hitting outfielder who had an excellent on-base percentage and terrific power numbers. During that 1975 campaign Carbo hit 15 home runs and had 50 RBIs in only 319 at-bats. He helped balance the Boston lineup.

Wise was later used in another deal meant to shore up Boston's starting rotation. He was sent to Cleveland in a package with Bo Diaz, Mike Paxton, and Ted Cox on March 30, 1978. In return, Boston received Dennis Eckersley and Fred Kendall. When the trade was made, Eckersley ranked with California's Frank Tanana and New York's Ron Guidry as the most gifted power pitchers in the league. Paxton and Cox did little for the Indians. Diaz, languishing behind Carlton Fisk, was several years away from an excellent career. Wise was at the end of one. Eckersley became the Red Sox ace and a 20-game winner. He helped bring them to within a playoff game of the pennant in 1978.

One of the more famous transactions in franchise history was a deal that wasn't consummated. On June 15, 1976, Boston purchased Joe Rudi and Rollie Fingers from the Oakland Athletics for $2 million. But it was a deal that wasn't. Rudi and Fingers had been stars with the champion A's. Left fielder Rudi was cited by Billy Martin as "a player without a weakness," and reliever Fingers had been the most intimidating member of baseball's most intimidating team. With Boston's offense sputtering and its bullpen a no-man's land, this deal would have turned the team around—and just imagine if Fingers had been with the club in 1978! Alas, it was vetoed by baseball commissioner Bowie Kuhn, who declared the transaction contrary to "the best interests of baseball." One wonders how he would have ruled had he been in office when the Red Sox sold Babe Ruth to the New York Yankees. That transaction started the decline of the once mighty Red Sox, made the Yankees a world-class power, and dramatically altered the history of baseball.

GREAT MOMENTS

It has been called by some the greatest World Series game ever played. When the Boston Red Sox and Cincinnati Reds took the field for the sixth game of the 1975 World Series, the Red Sox were perched on the edge of the abyss. After splitting the first four games, the Reds had used a three-run outburst in the sixth inning of Game 5 to take a one-game lead in the Series. One more Cincinnati win and the loyal Boston fans would have to face yet another winter of discontent.

Red Sox diehards often speak in hushed tones of the jinx that seems to dog their team. This is some vengeful spell that undoes all the promise of winning summers and that, at the most crucial moments, turns the sweet, heady brew of ultimate victory into the acid dregs of unfathomable loss. This time, however, the baseball muses seemed to side with the Sox.

It was an exhausted Boston team that had dropped Game 5 to Cincinnati. The club's starting rotation relied heavily on the arms of its Big Three: right-handers Luis Tiant and Rick Wise and left-hander Bill Lee. Each had pitched over 250 innings. Wise and Tiant especially had been taxed during the season's final weeks, when Boston once and for all shook off the pesky Baltimore Orioles. The 17-game-winning Lee had been unable to pitch in the playoffs. He had hyperextended his left arm and torn the small tendon in his elbow. As Lee later recalled, "I was virtually useless for those final four or five weeks. The injury didn't completely heal until just before the World Series started." That tear put an added burden on Wise and Tiant.

The two veterans were up to the challenge. They each won a game in the AL playoffs against Oakland. Tiant was magnificent in games 1 and 4 of the Series. He was awarded two complete-game victories. Wise, though, had been roughed up in Game 3. Having pitched well in Game 2, Lee would have pitched the sixth game.

The left-hander was one of the most respected competitors in the game despite a reputation as a baseball "flake." He had been a 17-game winner three years in a row. But there was hardly a fan in Beantown who didn't secretly wish for the crafty Tiant to be on the mound for what was now the season's most important game. Since he had pitched on October 15—and Game 6 was scheduled for October 18—there was no chance that this wish could be granted.

But then the rains came.

It didn't rain for forty days and forty nights, and none of the good people of Boston were seen building arks. It did, however, pour long enough to delay the resumption of the Series until October 21. This gave the Red Sox ample time to regroup and allowed El Tiante to once again toe the Fenway mound.

Since his 1972 return from arm problems, Tiant had been Boston's money pitcher. He was the guy fans and teammates wanted on the mound in a big game. And when the hometown nine scored three runs in the top of Game 6's first inning, the

Fenway faithful went wild. With Tiant on the mound, a seventh game now seemed inevitable.

The Reds, however, proved uncooperative. They scored three runs in the fifth inning to tie the game. Then the unthinkable happened. Having allowed two more runs to score in the seventh and yet another run on a lead-off homer in the eighth, Tiant, mighty Tiant, was taken out of the game. Boston reliever Roger Moret followed him to the mound. The Red Sox appeared to be doomed. With only six outs left to them, they were three runs behind what many people thought was baseball's best team, a club with the most balanced bullpen in the majors. Veteran relievers Clay Carroll and Pedro Borbon had already held the Sox scoreless in the fifth, sixth, and seventh. With rookies Rawley Eastwick (22 saves) and Will McEnaney (15 saves) ready and rested, the Cincinnati lead seemed insurmountable.

But it wasn't. Fred Lynn, the Boston center fielder who had been All-World in 1975 and who had hit a three-run homer in the game's first inning, continued to add to the grand memories of his historic rookie season by leading off the eighth with a single. Veteran third baseman Rico Petrocelli followed with a walk. The tying run came to the plate and Reds manager Sparky Anderson, known to his pitchers as "Captain Hook," went to his bullpen.

Eastwick took the mound. For the first two batters he seemed obdurate and invincible. Right fielder Dwight Evans, a particularly tough hitter at Fenway, fanned for the first out. Shortstop Rick Burleson, a gritty clutch performer all season, hit a harmless pop fly. Two outs, no runs. Left-handed pinch-hitter Bernie Carbo came to the plate. On the first pitch, he looked as if he would enjoy no more success than Evans or Burleson. Seemingly overmatched by Eastwick's velocity, Carbo flailed wildly and late at an inside fastball.

Pleased with his success, Eastwick tried to repeat it with another inside heater. This one, however, did not reach its intended destination. Veering slightly to the right, it wandered into the middle of the plate. Carbo's bat, quicker this time, intercepted it and sent the ball on a high parabola into the center-field bleachers. As soon as it left his bat, pandemonium broke loose. The game was tied.

After Boston right-hander Dick Drago held the Reds scoreless in the top of the ninth, his teammates almost settled matters in their half of the inning. They loaded the bases with none out, but second baseman Denny Doyle, attempting to score on a fly ball, was thrown out at the plate by left fielder George Foster. A third out sent the game into extra innings.

Drago pitched into and out of a jam in the 10th. Reds right-hander Pat Darcy blanked Boston in their half of that inning. Leading off top of the 11th, Pete Rose was hit by a Drago pitch. Cincinnati right fielder Ken Griffey, perhaps the best bunter in his league, laid one down to move Rose into scoring position. This was the moment of truth. Boston catcher Carlton Fisk, furiously pouncing on the ball, cooly decided to risk everything with a throw to second base. His rocket nipped Rose for a force-out. Fisk's choice changed the complexion of the inning and the game. The next bit of Boston heroics saved the evening.

Cincinnati second baseman Joe Morgan, baseball's best player, followed Griffey to the plate. He sent a Drago fastball into the night on a rising line that seemed destined to carry over the right-field fence. Disaster, which had ruined so many Red Sox parties in the past, was once again beckoning Boston to join it in a dance of death. Dwight Evans refused the invitation. The nonpareil right fielder was off at the crack of the bat. Though the ball had left the bat quickly, it lacked loft. To those watching from the stands, it now seemed as if it would hit off the fence. A double. It was clear that if Evans could get to the carom on time, his powerful right arm could still keep the Reds scoreless.

Evans had a better idea. Running as if his city's life depended on it, Evans sprinted backward, made a turn to his left, and essayed a last-second lunge for the screaming sphere. He caught it over his head at the fence. Morgan and the Reds had been denied. Not satisfied with merely making the best catch of the Series, Evans came up throwing and doubled Griffey off first. The inning was over. Evans's strikeout with the bases loaded in the 10th was forgiven and forgotten.

Right then you knew, you just *knew*, Boston was not going to lose this game. The Red Sox failed to score in the bottom of the 11th. Rick Wise held off the Reds in the top of the 12th.

Carlton Fisk led off the bottom of the 12th for Boston. From the moment Fisk had joined the Red Sox as a regular in 1972, the clubhouse atmosphere had undergone an amazing alchemy. Prior to his arrival, the Red Sox were thought of as underachievers, talented players who lacked motivation and leadership. Fisk changed that. Not too long into his rookie season he astounded teammates by lashing out at their complacency. He also took veterans Carl Yastrzemski and Reggie Smith to task for failing to lead. The club responded by playing its best ball of the summer; it came within a half game of winning the AL East. As Bill Lee later pointed out, "After Carlton spoke his piece, we discovered we had finally found a leader. And it was him."

Fisk thrived on pressure. No one on the club—not Yaz, not Petrocelli, not even the rookie wunderkinds Fred Lynn and Jim Rice—was better with the game on the line. Now he was up in a contest that held Boston's season in the balance.

Darcy was still on the mound. Fisk hit the right-hander's second pitch up into the darkness. There was no question that this ball was going to leave the park. But for an eternal half second, the players, the fans, and the 62 million television viewers held their collective breath and wondered if the ball would land foul or fair. Fisk was not holding his breath. Instead, he used a cosmic combination of desperate body language and every ounce of a will made hard by unforgiving Vermont winters to psychically coerce the ball into fair territory. His body weaved and waved as he stutter-stepped up the first-base line. The catcher's dance was not in vain. The ball hit the foul pole, just fair, just enough to land in the record books. Fisk jubilantly rounded the bases and jumped on home plate with both feet. The struggle was over.

The Red Sox had lived to play another game.

They didn't win that final contest the following night. With the score tied 3–3, Ken Griffey started the Cincinnati ninth with a walk off left-handed reliever Jim Burton. He moved to second on a sacrifice. Burton retired pinch-hitter Dan Driessen and intentionally walked Pete Rose. Joe Morgan came to the plate. With the count one-and-two, Burton threw an excellent down-and-away slider. Morgan couldn't get good wood on the pitch, but he got enough to dunk the ball into short center field. Griffey scored the last run of the season. The Red Sox were retired in the ninth. Boston fans wouldn't have a chance to see their heroes triumphantly douse themselves in champagne. They wouldn't have the pleasure of seeing a world championship flag fly over Fenway Park. They wouldn't have the morning papers greet them with that impossible bold, black headline "The Red Sox Win the Series!" But they had the sixth game. They would always have the sixth game.

Fisk Wins It!: Carlton Fisk's home run gives Boston a dramatic win in "the greatest world series game ever played" (October 21, 1975)

ALL TIME ALL STAR TEAM

CATCHER ★ CARLTON FISK

Catching had been an unstable Red Sox position for almost 20 years when Carlton Fisk joined the club for good in 1972. Once the job was in his capable mitts, however, Boston anxieties were relieved. Fisk won the Rookie of the Year and Gold Glove awards that season, batting .293 with 22 home runs. He also became a vocal leader in what had often been called a distracted clubhouse. Strong and durable, he holds the American League record for most games caught in a career. In 1987, he passed the 300 home-run mark, and in 1990 he became the all-time home-run leader among catchers. Slow and methodical, Fisk has been an outstanding handler of pitchers. His game-winning home run in Game 6 of the 1975 World Series remains one of baseball's most thrilling moments. He is a certain Hall of Famer.

FIRST BASE ★ JIMMIE FOXX

Double-X was an 11-year veteran when he joined the Red Sox in 1936. His glory years had been spent with Connie Mack's Philadelphia Athletics, but he still had enough left to win a home-run crown (1939). In his best Boston season (1938), Foxx hit 50 home runs, yet he was never really in the home-run race. He finished second to Detroit first baseman Hank Greenberg, who hit 58 and challenged Babe Ruth's record for most of that season. Foxx did lead the league in RBIs that year, with 175; batting average, with .349; and walks, with 119. He played six full seasons (1936–41) with the Red Sox. In that time he hit 217 home runs and amassed 774 RBIs.

SECOND BASE ★ BOBBY DOERR

From 1937 to 1951, with a year off in 1945, Bobby Doerr was the glue that held the Boston infield together. In 14 seasons he was named to the All-Star team nine times. In 1944 he led the AL in slugging and was named MVP. Doerr hit 223 home runs and had 1,247 RBIs. Much of that power could be attributed to his playing in Fenway Park, but he was also a run-producing threat on the road. His greatest asset, however, was his glove. During his major league tenure, he was the best fielding second baseman in baseball. In 1948, in a heated pennant race, Doerr went three months and 414 chances without an error.

SHORTSTOP ★ JOE CRONIN

Talk about rising through baseball's ranks! Cronin was an All-Star player, a pennant-winning manager, a general manager, and American League president. Like Jimmie Foxx, he was an established veteran when he joined Boston in 1935 as player-manager. He was the team's starting shortstop for seven years and drove in 100 or more runs three times. He topped the 90-RBI mark on three other occasions. In 1938 he led the league in doubles (51). Cronin benched himself after the 1941 season but remained on the roster, primarily as a pinch-hitter. He hit .429 as a pinch-hitter in 1943, leading the AL with 18 pinch-hits.

THIRD BASE ★ WADE BOGGS

The man with the magic wand bat. In just nine years, Boggs has placed himself among the legendary hitters of baseball. Though Ted Williams was the superior all-around hitter (Boggs can't hope to duplicate Williams's power), even the Splendid Splinter was unable to win four consecutive batting titles, as Boggs did from 1985 to 1988. When he first joined the club in 1982, Boggs was a man without a position. He shuttled back and forth from first base to third. He became the regular third baseman in 1983. Though unpolished at first, Boggs's defense has been of Gold Glove quality in recent years.

LEFT FIELD ★ TED WILLIAMS

Who else could keep Carl Yastrzemski off Boston's all-time team? Teddy Ballgame ranks barely below Babe Ruth as the greatest hitting force baseball has ever seen. He won six AL batting titles and was a perennial contender in those years when he didn't win. His other accomplishments include: four home-run titles, four RBI championships, eight-time leader in walks, six-time leader in runs scored, and nine slugging average titles. He led the AL in on-base percentage 12 times, seven times consecutively. His legendary .406 batting average in 1941 marked the last time any major leaguer has topped .400. Williams possessed the best batting eye in baseball. He walked 2,019 times and struck out only 709 times. Combined with a .634 slugging average, it made for a devastating package.

CENTER FIELD ★ TRIS SPEAKER

Speaker joined the Red Sox for good in 1909. In the era of the dead ball, he played the shallowest center field in baseball. At times he acted like a fifth infielder and was noted for making unassisted double plays on short fly balls. He was also the pivot man on many 4-8-3 double plays. (Try finding that notation on a scorecard today!) Speaker's great speed permitted him this luxury. Balls hit over his head were easily run down. He, Harry Hooper, and Duffy Lewis formed one of the greatest defensive outfields of all time. They helped lead the Red Sox to pennants in 1912 and 1915. An MVP in that first pennant-winning season, Speaker had a lifetime batting average of .344 and he stole 433 bases.

RIGHT FIELD ★ DWIGHT EVANS

At the end of the 1975 World Series, Cincinnati manager Sparky Anderson was appraising defeated Boston's roster. Eyeing the names of young phenoms Fred Lynn, Jim Rice, and Cecil Cooper, Sparky commented, "You know that Evans kid might end up putting up better numbers than any of them." Sparky was prescient. Dwight Evans has become one of baseball's superstars and an almost certain Hall of Famer. He finished his career with Boston in the top four in the following career departments: homeruns, RBI, games played, at-bats, runs, hits, doubles, total bases, extra-base hits, and walks. His bat alone would win him a place on this team, but he also happened to be the best right fielder in the AL throughout the 1980s. His arm rates with the greatest of all time: Furillo, Clemente, Ruth, Maris, Colavito, and Mays.

RIGHT-HANDED STARTER ★ ROGER CLEMENS

It didn't take long for the Rocket to join this elite group. Back-to-back Cy Young Awards (1986–87) almost guaranteed his inclusion, and his subsequent record has made the choice easy. Over the last five years he has been the best pitcher in baseball, compiling the best winning percentage, a low ERA, and league-leading strikeout totals—and in one of the worst pitcher's parks in baseball. His 20 strikeouts against the Seattle Mariners on April 20, 1986, remains a major league record for a nine-inning game.

LEFT-HANDED STARTER ★ BABE RUTH

If you could actually place this team on a Field of Dreams, just imagine the terror of the opposing pitcher, who would have to face Williams and Ruth in the same lineup. Do you think Ruth the pitcher would bat ninth? Hardly. Even as a pitcher for the Red Sox, the Babe was one of the league's most powerful hitters. And he was every bit as good on the mound. From 1915 to 1918 he won 78 games while losing only 40. He won the 1916 ERA title (1.75) and had a lifetime mark of 2.28. How good was Ruth the pitcher? Baseball historian Leonard Koppett once wrote, "He might have become the greatest of all . . . but baseball history would have been inconceivably different."

RELIEF PITCHER ★ DICK RADATZ

For four years (1962–65) the Monster terrorized American League hitters. He was the most feared relief pitcher in baseball. Throwing a fastball at speeds that had no place in time, Radatz was as close to untouchable as any pitcher who ever lived. Hitting against him as he lurked in the early evening shadows of Fenway Park was unfair. Pitching for poor teams, Radatz led the league in saves twice (1962, '64) and relief wins three times (1962, '63, '64). His strikeout totals were mind-boggling. During his four-year run, Radatz struck out 608 batters in 538 innings.

CAREER

BATTING

Games	Carl Yastrzemski	3,308
At-bats	Carl Yastrzemski	11,988
Batting average	Wade Boggs	.346
Runs	Carl Yastrzemski	1,816
Hits	Carl Yastrzemski	3,419
Doubles	Carl Yastrzemski	646
Triples	Harry Hooper	130
Home runs	Ted Williams	521
Grand slams	Ted Williams	17
Total bases	Carl Yastrzemski	5,539
Slugging percentage	Ted Williams	.634
RBIs	Carl Yastrzemski	1,844
Extra-base hits	Carl Yastrzemski	1,157
Bases on balls	Ted Williams	2,019
Strikeouts	Dwight Evans	1,559
Stolen bases	Harry Hooper	300

PITCHING

Games	Bob Stanley	637
Wins	Cy Young	192
Losses	Cy Young	112
Starts	Cy Young	297
Complete games	Cy Young	276
Shutouts	Cy Young	38
Innings	Cy Young	2,729.1
ERA	Smoky Joe Wood	1.99
Strikeouts	Roger Clemens	1,424
Walks	Mel Parnell	758
Saves	Bob Stanley	132
Relief appearances	Bob Stanley	552
Winning percentage	Roger Clemens	.695

Bob Stanley

Ted Williams

RECORD HOLDERS

SEASON

BATTING

Games	Jim Rice (1978)	163
At-bats	Jim Rice (1978)	677
Batting average	Ted Williams (1941)	406
Runs	Ted Williams (1949)	150
Hits	Wade Boggs (1985)	240
Doubles	Earl Webb (1931)	67
Triples	Tris Speaker (1913), Chick Stahl (1904)	22
Home runs	Jimmie Foxx (1938)	50
Grand slams	Babe Ruth (1919)	4
Total bases	Jim Rice (1978)	406
Slugging percentage	Ted Williams (1941)	.735
RBIs	Jimmie Foxx (1938)	175
Extra-base hits	Jimmie Foxx (1938)	92
Bases on balls	Ted Williams (1947, 1949)	162
Most strikeouts	Butch Hobson (1977)	162
Fewest strikeouts (500 ab)	Stuffy McInnis (1921)	9
Stolen bases	Tommy Harper (1973)	54

PITCHING

Games	Dick Radatz (1964)	79
Wins	Smoky Joe Wood (1912)	34
Losses	Red Ruffing (1928)	25
Starts	Cy Young (1902)	43
Complete games	Cy Young (1902, 1904)	41
Shutouts	Cy Young (1904), Joe Wood (1912)	10
Innings	Cy Young (1902)	385
ERA	Dutch Leonard (1914)	1.01
Strikeouts	Roger Clemens (1988)	291
Walks	Mel Parnell (1949)	134
Saves	Bob Stanley (1983)	33
Relief appearances	Dick Radatz (1964)	79
Winning percentage	Bob Stanley (1978)	15-2, .882

TRIVIA QUIZ

1. What St. Louis Cardinal broke up Jim Lonborg's no-hitter in the eighth inning of the second game of the 1967 World Series?

2. Carl Yastrzemski was a Triple Crown winner and the MVP in 1967. Only one other player received a first-place vote in the MVP balloting that year. Who was that player?

3. Who was the winning pitcher when Carlton Fisk hit his game-winning homer in the sixth game of the 1975 World Series?

4. What ill-fated Red Sox first baseman was known as the "Golden Greek"?

5. Who was the first Red Sox player to win a batting title?

6. Who was the losing pitcher when Enos Slaughter made his mad dash for home as the Cardinals beat Boston in Game 7 of the 1946 World Series?

7. What right-hander went 12-2 in his rookie year with the Red Sox and then never enjoyed another winning season?

8. The 1950 Red Sox hit .302 as a team. Who were the only two regulars with batting averages below .300?

9. Only four Red Sox pitchers have ever led the league in strikeouts. Name them.

10. The Red Sox forced the Cardinals to use eight pitchers in Game 6 of the 1967 World Series. Name them.

ANSWERS ON PAGE 63

1991 SCHEDULE

APRIL

SUN	MON	TUE	WED	THU	FRI	SAT
	1	2	3	4	5	6
7	8 TOR 2:05	9 TOR 7:35	10 TOR 7:35	11 CLE 1:05	12	13 CLE 1:05
14 CLE 1:05	15 CLE 11:05	16 KC 1:05	17 KC 1:05	18 KC 1:05	19 CLE 7:35	20 CLE 1:35
21 CLE 1:35	22 TOR 7:35	23 TOR 7:35	24 TOR 6:05	25	26 KC 8:35	27 KC 2:35
28 KC 8:05	29	30 MIN 8:05				

MAY

SUN	MON	TUE	WED	THU	FRI	SAT
			1 MIN 8:35	2	3 CHI 8:05	4 CHI 7:05
5 CHI 3:15	6	7 MIN 7:35	8 MIN 7:35	9 TEX 7:35	10 TEX 7:35	11 TEX 3:05
12 TEX 1:05	13 CHI 7:35	14 CHI 7:35	15 CHI 7:35	16	17 TEX 8:35	18 TEX 8:35
19 TEX 3:05	20 MIL 7:35	21 MIL 7:35	22 MIL 6:05	23 DET 7:35	24 DET 7:35	25 DET 7:35
26 DET 1:35	27 NY 1:05	28 NY 7:30	29 NY 7:30	30 BAL 7:35	31 BAL 7:35	

JUNE

SUN	MON	TUE	WED	THU	FRI	SAT
						1 BAL 1:05
2 BAL 1:05	3	4 CAL 10:35	5 CAL 10:35	6 CAL 10:35	7 OAK 10:35	8 OAK 4:05
9 OAK 4:05	10 SEA 10:05	11 SEA 10:35	12 SEA 3:35	13	14 CAL 7:35	15 CAL 1:05
16 CAL 1:05	17 CAL 7:35	18 SEA 7:35	19 SEA 7:35	20 OAK 7:35	21 OAK 7:35	22 OAK 1:05
23 OAK 1:05	24	25 NY 7:35	26 NY 7:35	27 NY 7:35	28 BAL 7:35	29 BAL 1:15
30 BAL 1:35						

☐ Home games   ☐ Road games

JULY

SUN	MON	TUE	WED	THU	FRI	SAT
	1 MIL 8:35	2 MIL 8:35	3 MIL 8:35	4 DET 6:05	5 DET 7:35	6 DET 1:05
7 DET 1:05	8	9 ALL-STAR GAME	10	11 MIN 8:05	12 MIN 8:05	13 MIN 8:05
14 MIN 2:05	15 CHI 8:05	16 CHI 8:05	17 CHI 8:05	18 MIN 7:35	19 MIN 7:35	20 MIN 1:05
21 MIN 1:05	22 TEX 8:35	23 TEX 8:35	24 TEX 8:35	25	26 CHI 7:35	27 CHI 1:05
28 CHI 8:05	29 TEX 7:35	30 TEX 1:05	31 OAK 7:35			

AUGUST

SUN	MON	TUE	WED	THU	FRI	SAT
				1 OAK 7:35	2 TOR 7:35	3 TOR 1:15
4 TOR 1:05	5 KC 8:35	6 KC 8:35	7 KC 8:35	8	9 TOR 7:35	10 TOR 1:35
11 TOR 1:35	12 TOR 7:35	13 CLE 7:35	14 CLE 7:35	15 CLE 7:35	16 KC 7:35	17 KC 1:05
18 KC 1:05	19 CLE 7:35	20 CLE 7:35	21 CLE 6:05	22	23 CAL 10:35	24 CAL 10:05
25 CAL 4:05	26 OAK 10:05	27 OAK 10:05	28 OAK 3:15	29	30 SEA 10:35	31 SEA 10:05

SEPTEMBER

SUN	MON	TUE	WED	THU	FRI	SAT
1 SEA 8:05	2	3 CAL 7:35	4 CAL 7:35	5 SEA 7:35	6 SEA 7:35	7 SEA 1:05
8 SEA 1:05	9	10 DET 7:35	11 DET 7:35	12 NY 7:30	13 NY 7:30	14 NY 1:30
15 NY 8:05	16 BAL 7:35	17 BAL 7:35	18 BAL 6:05	19	20 NY 7:35	21 NY 3:15
22 NY 1:05	23 BAL 7:35	24 BAL 7:35	25 BAL 7:35	26	27 MIL 8:35	28 MIL 2:35
29 MIL 2:35	30 MIL 8:35					

OCTOBER

SUN	MON	TUE	WED	THU	FRI	SAT
		1 DET 7:35	2 DET 7:35	3 DET 7:35	4 MIL 7:35	5 MIL 1:05
6 MIL 1:05	7	8	9	10	11	12

COLLECTOR'S CORNER

NOTES
&
AUTOGRAPHS

Ain't no fences high enough.

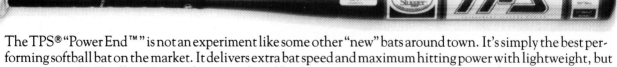

The TPS® "Power End™" is not an experiment like some other "new" bats around town. It's simply the best performing softball bat on the market. It delivers extra bat speed and maximum hitting power with lightweight, but super-strong CU31 alloy. No wonder it's preferred by the most powerful hitters in the game. Better get one, while the fences last.